Life After Death
A Widow's Journey

By
Lynn Davis

A Guide to
Starting Over

It starts with a knock at the door or waking up to find your husband slumped over and blue at the kitchen table. That is the beginning of the nightmare. The shock of the moment scrambles all of your senses and you can't think. Over the last 10 years I have lost two immediate members of my family. There were times I just don't know if I wanted to go on. I lost my husband last year but the worst was my son 10 years ago. Both deaths had some things that were similar but losing a child and a spouse were very different.

I have written this book and included examples of both in hopes it will help you in your time of need. I have put in lines so that you can enter information, contact numbers and/or just to write down a list of things to assist you.

Your Loss

I woke up late and went to see why my husband let me sleep in so late. I found him slumped over at the kitchen table. He had been of poor health for quite some time but I still didn't register what I was seeing. I picked him up and put him on the floor. He wasn't breathing and his face was blue and cold to the touch. I administered CPR and talked to 911 at the same time. The Fire Department was right around the corner and was at my house is just a few minutes. He had had a massive heart attack and was already dead when I found him. I shouldn't have slept in and kept beating myself up that I wasn't with him when he needed me most. The police captain told me even if I had been sitting right next to him it would not have helped.

My son's death was the hardest thing I have ever had to go through. My nightmare started with a knock at the door at 10:00 PM. I thought Chris had forgot his key again. Through the curtains I could see the flashing lights of a police car. "Oh no, now what has he done," I thought. My husband and I got out of bed and opened the front door to the police office and coroner. Chris died in an auto accident. My family and friends helped me through a time I didn't want to go on living. We were living in Ohio at that time. After telling my daughter and mother they booked the first flight out. They took charge and I couldn't have made it without them.

Calling Family and Friends - With any death there is always the heart breaking task of calling family and friends. When my husband died there were fire trucks, police and finally the funeral van to pick up his body. My neighbors came over and stayed with me while the police and coroner were investigating. Once they left I started making the calls.

Immediate family_____

Your supervisor at work _____

The deceased person's work supervisor_____

Lawyer (if needed) _____

Close family friends_____

When my son died all of my family flew in along with some of our friends. I had to call my work to let them know I wouldn't be in, as well as my son's work place. One thing about living in a small town, news gets around fast. The first time I had seen the crash site was when we turned on the news channel. It was showing pictures of the wreck every 15 minutes. Within a half an hour I had a house full of people trying to help and asking questions that I couldn't even think how to answer. I was barely functioning. My son worked for Panera Bread and his supervisor as well as some of his co-workers arrived an hour after I had called them with the news. They brought in platters of food. The ladies from my work arrived shortly after with more food.

After the initial wave of visitors left, we had a couple of hours before we had to start picking up family members. Just looking around I had my husband drive me to Walmart to pick up more pillows, towels, food and drinks. I cried up and down all the aisles but it got me away from the house for a few minutes. If you will be having out of town guests see if you can get someone to assist you with the following:

Nearest Hotel Information_____

Who will need to be picked if traveling by air _____

Flight number and time of arrival_____

Rental Car Agency_____

List of basic supplies for out of town guests, i.e., pillows, blankets, food, toilet paper, clean towels, boxes of tissues _____

If you are unable to drive have another family assist you. Write down a list for them to follow.

It was sometimes overwhelming when food and flowers started coming in. If there was a card with the flowers, I wrote a brief description on the back so I could write out thank you letters later. We also received cards with money in them for funeral expenses. On the back of each card I wrote down the amount. I kept some of the envelopes that had addresses on them that weren't in my address book for the thank you notes. For the food from neighbors and friends I had a note pad to jot down notes:

Food _____

Flowers_____

Gifts_____

Cash_____

Donations/Charity_____

Family Doctor - My husband called our doctor to have him prescribe something to calm me down. Basically I was a walking zombie but it helped me get through the first couple of weeks. When my husband died I decided I wouldn't take any medication and after the first week I was able to make it through the day but nights were hard.

Family Doctor _____

Pharmacy _____

With both deaths I just didn't want to eat or drink anything for the first week. My daughter finally got me to eat a piece of chocolate cake one of my friends had made. Thinking back, I think I had cake for breakfast, lunch and dinner for the first week. With my husband's death I picked up some Ensure shakes which was about all I could get down. My daughter and her family were on vacation in Canada when my husband died. She flew back in to help out. She would pester me until I would try and eat something. In order to get through this difficult time you need to take care of yourself so that you can take care of your family.

My husband was scheduled for surgery within a few days of his death. I had to call and cancel all of those appointments and notify the hospital to cancel the surgery. If your family member have doctor appointments you will need to notify them.

Doctors_____

Hospital_____

Cardiologist _____

Due to some of the pain pills my husband was taking the police actually counted the medication to make sure he had not overdosed. Ask the police what are the procedure(s) to get rid of the prescription medications.

Call pharmacy to cancel auto-renewal of medications_____

Make a list of all medications your family takes on a regular basis. I had to scramble to find all of his medications and answer questions when I was still in shock that he was really gone.

Police, Coroner & Grief Counselor - A grief counselor arrived shortly after the coroner had pronounced my husband dead. The lady was very nice and gave me some guides on dealing with my loss and asked where I would like to take him. She made the arrangements to have him picked up by the mortuary. She stayed for a couple of hours until the police and coroner had left.

Police/Coroner Case Number: _____

Police Contact Information: _____

Coroner Contact Information: _____

When my son passed away our lawyer gave me the name of a counselor that dealt with children's deaths. I went but it was just too much for me to have to talk to the counselor about my feelings. With my son's death there were also legal issues that I had to work through. I did go back to the counselor after a couple of weeks but I would cry through all of the sessions. I don't know if it helped or hurt. Sometimes our brains will block out traumatic events like a death. I know what basically happened that first week but the faces and names along with viewing him in the casket are behind a door in my brain that I was not able to open. At first I thought I was going crazy but the counselor did tell me that this is a reaction to help us get through tragic events. To this day that door has remained shut but now I am alright to leave it that way.

Legal Assistance - When my son passed away we were instructed by the police officer to retain a lawyer due to the violent nature of his passing. We received a reference to an attorney from my mother-in-law's family lawyer. To our surprise the lawyer arrived at our house within an hour of the call. He was able to prioritize what was needed and advise us our next steps.

The lawyer took care of the press who arrived at the house shortly after he arrived. We had two different news vans that had parked in the grass of our front yard and reporters at the front door with camera crews.

Daily Diary – Our lawyer advised me to start writing down everything from who I spoke with, to medication taken daily. I didn't release how helpful this really became until I looked back over the last couple of weeks of notes and realized how much I couldn't remember. I kept the diary going for the next year. This was extremely helpful for the trial but also for taking care of taxes for the next year.

My son was 19 years and had no Will. Our lawyer was able to have me appointed by the court as Administrator of his estate even though he had less than a dollar in the bank. Here is some of the information I recorded:

Daily medication and dosage_____

Who I spoke with and brief summary of conversation_____

_____

Don't forget the date and time_____

Did you work or took the day off – record time off of work as well_____

Keep receipts for parking and mileage for doctor or hospital visits.

The lawyer had set up an accordion folder with tabs for doctor visits, expenses, lawyer, police reports, and cards from family and friends, etc. It took two and half years to close his estate. Even after everything was finished I still have all of the documents together and every once in a while I have to go and find something.

Organ Donor Program – While my husband and lawyer were trying to deal with the press, I received a phone call from the Organ Donor Program representative. My son had checked the box on the application for his driver's license to be an Organ Donor. I had completely forgotten and wasn't ready for all the questions about his medical history. I did my best to give them information on his general health and approved the donation.

Organ Donor contact_____

Phone number and address of facility_____

As hard as this is to do, you will need to have this discussion with your remaining family members. It was heart breaking to even talk to the organ donor representative, when I was still trying to cope with the fact that I wouldn't see him again. I was in denial that first week. The donation was able to save three different lives. I received a medal and donor lapel pins from the Organ Donor Company and was invited to write something about Chris and they posted it on their website.

Write down family members and decision to donate   or not_____

Making Funeral Arrangements

This should be discussed ahead of time with family. No matter how hard this discussion is to have, it will help you know how to handle their wishes. This is the last thing I would have ever discussed with my son. I always thought I would be the first to go. When we went to the funeral home my mother and husband took over. You will need to take clothing of the deceased if you have an open casket. I couldn't believe how expensive everything was. I was in a panic on how to pay for this. Fortunately I had help for my family. My son's funeral cost $8,000. This is some of what you will need to decide for the funeral.

Funeral   Home   Phone
Number_____

Funeral Home Address_____

Date of service_____

Times for viewing/service_____

Will there by a grave side service_____

Minister/clergy_____

Guest book_____

Casket/cremation_____

Music for service_____

Pallbearers_____

Notice in newspaper - make sure you ask ahead of time. Prices differ and it can become quite costly.

After going through my son's funeral, my husband and I talked about what we wanted when our time came. We also started saving so that we would never have to ask for help when our time came. Little did I know that just 8 years later I would be saying goodbye to my husband who was only 54 years old. My husband had wanted to be cremated and have his ashes scattered into the ocean off of

Dana Point, California. My daughter and son-in-law took paddle boards out to the other side of the jetty. They waived when in position while my grandchildren and I put yellow roses in the surf to say goodbye. There was a lady with a camera watching us. One of the yellow roses washed up against a rock. When I went to pick it up she asked what we were doing. I explained to her about my husband and his wishes. She was so touched that she said she wanted the same when it was her time. There is no right and wrong way to say goodbye but just try and honor their last wishes.

Order 10 – 15 death certificates - You will need these for life insurance policies, change bank accounts, transferring title on cars, house, utilities, etc. Even after a year the IRS still had me send one with the tax return.

Ordering flowers for the service - Sometimes a family member will want to take care of this or you can pick them out yourself. After the funeral when everyone went home, I had plants and flowers everywhere. It was really hard to look at them without crying. We loaded up my husband's truck and took them to the nursing home. We asked if they could pass them out to some of their patients who didn't get visitors. They were delighted to get them. If you would prefer not to have any plants or flowers you can have family and friends donate to your favorite charity. For my son's half-sister who died in an accident, I sent a tree for them to plant in her honor.

Florist Phone Number and Address_____

Charity Name and Address_____

Hospital or Nursing Home_____

The Funeral - My son's funeral was held in a small town in southwest, Ohio. My family has a farm in the area and my grandparents and other family members were buried in the town's cemetery. It was a 45 minute drive from where we were living at the time so I didn't expect to see anyone other than family there. To my surprise there were 25 of his friends from school along with half of the town who knew my parents. The principle of the high school had excused my son's friends and arranged to have a grief counselor for any of the students that needed it.

We arrived at the funeral home one hour ahead of time. This was the first time I saw him. They gave me a few minutes before letting anyone else in. It didn't look like him. It looked like a wax figure of him. His spirit was gone. His friends left him notes, flowers and gifts. My daughter helped put together a board with pictures of him and his friends. I delivered the eulogy which was all the greatest adventures that Chris had. The funny stories and how he loved life. If you ever have to deliver a speech just look at a few people and pretend they are the only ones there. I spoke to my family and his friends. It was the only way I could get through it. I have it written down what I said but haven't read it since. My daughter got up and read a poem she wrote about Chris. The minister was a friend of my husband and mostly spoke to the kids, not the typical eulogy but it was perfect.

Eulogy/speakers_____

Arrange for flowers to be transported to grave side/house_____

Wake - For both my husband and son I had food ready for after the funeral. Everyone wanted to help out and I let them. My friends from work, neighbors and their friends all brought over food which turned into a giant pot luck.

Food/pot luck contribution_____

Be strong for your children - No matter who in your life has passed on, if have small children they will need you to help them understand what his happened. At my son's funeral the minister stayed at the grave side and answered questions for over an hour from some of my son's friends. For some of these teens it was the first time they were exposed to a death of a friend. After the funeral my son's friends came to our home and they gathered in the living room and put on Chris' favorite movie. They didn't make a sound. When the movie was over they hugged us and left. If there was an upside to his death it was the effect the funeral had on his friends and their vision for the future. Chris and his friends would party and just barely pass their classes in high school. After he was gone his closest friends refocused their lives and continued on to college or trade schools.

A Tribute from his friends - His friends had requested that the city put a plaque on the bench at the new skate park where Chris would sit and watch his friends on their skate boards. They camped out at city hall until the plaque was finally approved. I didn't know any of this was going on until the plaque was ready and the city made the presentation and all of his friends showed up. It was very touching. The local Surf/Skate shop mounted his skate board above their door for all of his friends.

Don't forget your pets - My husband had a dachshund that was his shadow. The last few years Brutus was never far from him. When I found Jim slumped over, Brutus was guarding his body. I had to put him in a kennel until the police had left. Over the next couple of days he wouldn't eat and he was searching for him. I bought him some special treats and took more time with him until he started to act normal again. He is now my shadow except when the grandchildren come over. That is when he acts like a puppy again.

After the Funeral - After the first week the guests started to leave and it went from total chaos to no noise at all. I would go around and turn on the TV because I couldn't stand the silence. It was time to go back to work. My friends and co-workers had all said how sorry they were and went back to their desk. At first I thought it was just me but they avoided me for a couple of weeks. I finally had to ask what was going on. My friend told me that they were all afraid of making me cry again.

To function I buried myself in work. Lessons learned: it is alright to not wear make-up. I would tough it out and learned how not to breakdown at work. I saved the tears for when I would be at home.

Driving - It was hard to keep the tears back and my mind focused while driving. I would be on my way to work, start looking around and couldn't figure out where I was or how I got there. This happened more than a few times. Listening to music I would associate different songs with events of the past and it would make me even cry more. To keep my mind focused I started listening to books on CD. We picked up some of my favorite authors and I began to listen and concentrate on the stories. Needless to say I built up quite a library. After a while I was able to listen to music again.

Cleaning out the wardrobe - A couple of weeks after the funeral my daughter came over to start helping me go through my husband's clothes and get them ready to donate. Write down how many shirts, pants, jackets, etc. so you will have the record for your taxes. Make sure you get a tax receipt from the charity. You don't have to do this all at once. I would work on one room at a time.

Name of Charity and address_____

Number and condition of the clothes_____

Date of donation_____

For my son's clothing I invited some of his friends over and told them they could have whatever they wanted. Four of his friends came over and started going through his clothes. They would pick up a shirt and tell me a story about when he last wore it. There were also some that the kids picked up a shirt and said "I have been looking for this." I think it helped both the kids and myself to walk memory lane for just a little while. The kids took about half of his clothing and I donated the rest to the church.

Losing friends - After 25 years of marriage we had lots of friends but most of them were his. For the first couple of months they would check in but after that one by one they all stopped calling or coming over. I was a little surprised but understood that being at our house was like rubbing salt in a wound. If this happens to you just remember - it's not you!

Thank you notes - Keep a list of gifts, flowers and cash that you receive, try and write out thank you cards within the first couple of weeks. Use that list to write out Christmas cards. I can't even look at those cards but they helped me through and it is hard to actually send out cards but it helped me move on.

Starting Over

The Blessing of Grandchildren

After dealing with my son's death it is hard to smile. That all changed when my daughter told me I was going to be a grandmother. The timing couldn't have been better. No one in our family had smiled in two years. That little bundle of joy brought smiles and healing back to the family. Milena squeezed my finger and restarted my heart again. Two years later her little brother Dorian was born. Watching them grow up has given my life a new focus. I truly enjoy having them over for a slumber party. Seeing life through their eyes is such a joy it takes you back to the time when my children were little. Embrace your inner child and look at the world through their eyes.

Insurance

Auto Insurance – When I took my husband off the policy they barely lowered the price of my policy. He had an accident but I was accident free and had no tickets for the last 25 years. When I pointed this out they lowered the policy a little more. It was time to start getting quotes from other insurance companies. The auto insurance we had at the time of my son's death actually paid the first $2,500 of funeral costs. This came up as a claim and I had to explain it was due to a death. They were surprised that we even knew about that clause in the insurance documents. Read your policy, not many have that clause but it really helped out when we were trying to figure out how to pay for the funeral. I asked three different insurance agents for quotes on the auto and house insurance policies.

Insurance agent & number_____

Quotes   –   Insurance   agency   &
cost_____

2nd Quote_____

3rd Quote_____

Life insurance – if you have a policy on the person who has passed away, the insurer will need an original death certificate. The mortuary can work with the insurance company to put a lien against the policy to pay for the funeral cost. Make sure you have a copy of the contact information on your life insurance policy. If the policy is from your work call the Human Resources department. They will help you get the process moving.

Insurance settlement – If you receive a settlement do not tell how much you are receiving or you will have lots of people ready to help you spend it. If you are asked you can tell them it was just enough to cover the expenses. Don't make any large purchases for a while. With my husband's death the policy covered the expenses with a little extra for emergencies. Over the course of the next year I am still receiving bills from various doctors and laboratories.

Beneficiary for Life Insurance policy – you will need to change any life insurance policies. If this isn't done ahead of time and there is another death the insurance company will hold up payment until after probate has been completed which could be a year or two. With the corrected Life Insurance Beneficiary form the claim can be processed as soon as they receive a certified Death Certificate.

Contact insurance agent_____

If you have a policy through your employer or his, contact Human Resources _____

Financial - Do you take care of the finances for your family or did your spouse? I can't tell you how many people I have known who don't have the slightest clue how to pay the bills, budget and take care of the financial matters for their family. I knew one woman that had never written a check or balanced her checkbook. If you don't know what to do start with taking a trip to your bank. When I first started working, the first 12 years was working in the Savings & Loan industry. We would sit with customers to show them how to balance a check book or try at least to make heads or tails of their check register. If you're computer savvy there are quite a few user friendly programs to help out. For those of you who are not then don't panic. My mother has never touched a computer and she has a check off list that is in a note book of what income coming in from Social Security and my dad's retirement at the top of the page then her normal monthly bills. She checks off the bills as they come in and writes down how much the bill was. Start by going through your normal bills and start making a list of how much is spent each month.

After making a list of income and expenses, do you have enough income to stay in your home or apartment? If not, then take a look at what you really need to get by. Start cutting out expenses to just the bare basics. If you own your home think about renting out a room to help with expenses. Someone you know or recommended by your family or co-workers is the best. Make sure to get references if renting to a stranger. Many of the colleges and senior centers will have bulletin boards where you can post a sign. Before the person moves in make sure to spell out exactly what will be charged.

Child(ren) and age(s) _____

Amount of rent and due date_____

Security Deposit_____

Pets _____

Share utility cost_____

Allow   friends   over   and curfew_____

Chores for common areas, i.e., bathroom cleaning, picking up after themselves, laundry, buying their own soap or sharing the costs.

Banks, Loans and Credit Card

Bank Accounts – I went into the bank with the death certificate in hand and the manager was very helpful. They scanned it in and attached it to our account. I kept my husband on the account until the next year so there wouldn't any issues with depositing our tax return. I did take his name off my checks.

Bank name and address_____

Checking accounts_____

Saving accounts_____

401(k) or Roth Accounts_____

Check on automatic payments_____

Check for on-line accounts_____

Credit cards_____

Credit Cards and loans – You might have to re-establish a credit line with some credit card companies. My husband and I cut up our credit cards. If we wanted something that wasn't in the budget we would have to save up. This will cut down impulse buying. My daughter was teaching my granddaughter, Milena, about the difference between needing something and wanting something. Milena (5 years old) turned the tables on her when my daughter found a cute dress. Milena looked at her mother and asked, "Now do you need that or want it?" My daughter walked away, aren't kids great!

Internet Accounts & Loans – When I first tried to clean up the mess, there were over 1,500 emails on my husband's computer to go through. Out of those emails I found out about a loan for things he had purchased on eBay. After my husband passed away I found out he had taken out a loan from PayPal for $800. I paid off the loan and started going through everything else in his office. For all of those junk emails on his email I changed them to junk and was able to block quite a few. Don't get rid of separate email accounts for a while. I also found out about automatic payments taken out of a separate internet bank account. It took months to clean up the mess.

Beneficiary Forms – you will need to change these on any 401(k), Roth accounts, stock, bonds, etc.

Changing your bills

Utilities – my husband had set up all of the utilities at our new home. Some of the utilities had asked for a copy of the death certificate in order to change the account to my name.

Electric Company_____

Propane_____

Gas Company_____

Water_____

Cable Company_____

Trash Pick-up day and time_____

Home owner association_____

Any lake or club memberships_____

Mortgage/Title to any property you held together – I hired a lawyer to take care of this and didn't do my homework and was taken for $1,500. The lawyer had rented space and it looked legitimate but he wouldn't return my calls or emails. It would cost even more to take him to court to get my money back. I did file a grievance with the bar association. I am working directly with the Mortgage Company to change the title. I may have to get another attorney to straighten everything out but this time I will make sure to do my homework.

Taxes

IRS – Prior to my spouses death we had found out someone had used his Social Security number to file a tax return and the IRS had already paid that person. We had to have the police file a report and check our identification to verify who we were. A month after we started the process of fixing that mess he passed away. Dealing with the IRS on this fraud claim was bad enough but throw in a death and it turned into a nightmare that is still going on. I finally got the tax return back but for the next 5 years I have to send all my returns to the IRS fraud division for special handling.

State Taxes - Our State taxes were easy for last year since we submitted them prior to my husband's death. This year I thought I would have issues but was able to file electronically. I used Turbo Tax software for both Federal and State. Even with his death the program will ask questions and steer you in the right direction.

Computers – Do you have all of your spouse or family member's passwords? My husband was very good at writing down passwords for the various programs he had on his computer. Unfortunately near the end his hand writing was very poor and hard to read. When contacting the companies they all wanted death certificates faxed to them, they wouldn't accept an email copy. I ran back and forth to the UPS store quite a bit.

Taking over your spouse's duties

When you lose a spouse you never really know how much then did and you took for granted. Some of the easiest things like light bulbs won't change themselves. Changing the batteries in your smoke detector need to be checked. Even the simplest of chores are hard to remember. After my husband's death I would forget to feed the dog until he finally started barking and picked up his bowl.   Make a list of daily chores, feeding pets, making sure they had enough water, picking up the mail and newspaper.   I put the list on my refrigerator so that I would get used to picking up the extra responsibilities I now had.

Trash cans - The first time I took out the trash I had no idea that there was a six foot long king snake living in that area. I started to move the trash can and saw the snake. It took off one way and I took off with the dog in the opposite direction. I called my son-in-law and told him what happened. I had him laughing on the phone. King snakes are very good to have around because they kill rattlesnakes. I moved the trash cans to the other side of the house and haven't see the snake again.

Car wash and maintenance – Hopefully you have friends or family who can assist with some the easy things like changing the oil and basic maintenance. Two months after my husband's death I had a flat tire. Luckily my son-in-law hadn't left for work yet and came over and changed the tire to the little emergency tire that was in the back of my car. At lunch I went over to a tire store close to my work and ended up buying two new tires and had them check and balance the others.

Gas Leak –Last week I opened the back door to let my dog out and was hit with a very strong smell. I got my son-in-law on the phone and he told me where to turn off the gas line to the barbeque. The cover was over the barbeque and when I took it off I got a face full of gas. We had heavy winds the previous last week the wind had pushed the barbeque into a tree branch that pushed the dial to medium. As soon as I turned it off the gas sound quit. I was very lucky and could have lost everything. The gas line was not capped and I had a lesson on how to turn off the outside gas and the water heater. I just received the gas bill and it was triple the normal cost.

Location and procedure to turn off the gas_____

Learn how to turn off the water in the event of a flood. If there is a problem with sprinklers make sure you know where to turn those off until you can get help repairing them. A small leak can send your water bill through the roof.

Location and procedure_____

Electric Breakers - Learn how to turn off breakers and if there isn't a clear chart attached make one so if there is a problem you will be able to easily be able to locate the correct breaker.

Location_____

Label Breakers_____

Power Outage – My husband was always preparing for a disaster. One day he hammered nails by each door in the house and hung little flashlights next to them. Since he would be up and around during the night I thought that was the reason. But when we had a power outage for 18 hours I found them to be very useful. After the power came back on I purchased some flameless tea lights. These are much safer than candles.

When we lived in Ohio there was a power outage during the winter. The temperature outside was at 20 degrees and inside with the fireplace going non-stop it was at 40 degrees. Each year we would always buy a joint gift for our anniversary. When the anniversary came along I asked for a generator. That little generator was great and we were able to keep the refrigerator running, heat the house and keep my hair dryer working. During the summer he would also take it along to the job site so that he could heat up his lunch in a microwave he had in the back of his truck. Naturally when the power went out last week the generator was being used by my son-in-law. Guess what he is getting for his birthday this year??

When Japan had their nuclear disaster my spouse ordered enough sodium iodine tablets for our family on the internet. I rolled my eyes at this one but it made him feel more secure. He liked to listen to talk radio and they were stated that it would slow down the radiation from getting into your system. Whether that is true or not I don't know.

NOAA Weather Radio – Voyager KA500 – solar & crank weather alert multiband radio with cell phones, MP3/IPOD charger - I found this one on the internet. My daughter's family liked to go camping each summer. I thought this would be a great gift for them. The package came in the mail and when I got home from work my husband was already playing with it. We ended up ordering one for us. It is very easy to use and we both tested it out. If there is an emergency at least we would be able to keep our cell phones and other devices charged.

Home Maintenance - Purchase a basic house maintenance book. I bought the book, 1001 Do-It-Yourself Hints & Tips at Barnes & Nobles. The book is great as it had all types of helpful tips for maintenance around the house along with pictures and diagrams on shutting off utilities. A book like this would assist you in determining if this is something you can handle or if you need to call in help.

Contractor - If you have to call in a contractor make sure to check out to make sure he has a contractor's license bond and get references. Make sure to get a written quote before any work can be started. If it is an expensive repair make sure to get multiple quotes before you agree to anything. If the contractor wants the entire cost up front that is a red flag.

Plants and Yard – My husband was a great gardener and took care of the lawn. I have the worst brown thumb ever. I even kill cactus. The first time he went in to the hospital I had to mow the lawn for the first time. He had just purchased a new lawn mower. I got it started, how hard would this be, I went 5 feet and smoke started billowing out of the engine. I called my son-in-law and he came over and found a bad seal in the motor. He was able to have the lawn mower replaced and finished the lawn mowing.

We have a large slope behind my house where my husband had my son-in-law terrace the slope and put twenty fruit trees, grape arbors, kiwi arbors and passion fruit. Just maintaining the orchard is a huge job so I have some gardeners come in quarterly to help out. Just weeding alone is a full time job. My son-in-law has a construction business which is a blessing. He is a great guy and is always there to help out. If he wasn't here I would be in a lot of trouble.

Safety – Now that you are alone you need to think about your safety at home and when you are out. My little dog barks if anyone walks who walk on the sidewalk. My husband had already install locks on the windows. I used to keep the kitchen door open so that Brutus could go outside in the evenings. I was reading a book and I looked up and there was a bobcat sitting right next to Brutus. Brutus is such a good watch dog, he was snoring. I got up slowly and started shoeing it out. The bobcat got up looked around and left. A couple of weeks later I had the door open and the bobcat came in the house again. My tough guard dog was four paws up sound asleep. The bobcat looked around and left. I told my next door neighbor about the bobcat and she laughed. The bobcat was domesticated and lived across the street. After a while Bobbi, the bobcat, even came up to me for some pets. I live in an area that there are a lot of coyotes and every once in a while a mountain lion. Even with a fenced backyard I only let Brutus out when I am around and outside with him. I started keeping the back door shut even when I was at home. You should also lock your front door and you have a garage door make sure to keep that locked as well. I would put my cell phone on the charger in the kitchen each night before I went to bed. If I was asleep Jim would get it since he was always roaming around all night. After his death I moved the charger next to my bed.

Self-defense class – Before I met my husband I had been attacked by someone who broke into my apartment. I never wanted to be that helpless again and signed up for a self-defense class for women that was taught at the local college. If you have the opportunity to take a class like this please sign up. You don't have to be a black belt the class teaches how to get out of a bad situation just using your body, keys and pepper spray. I haven't had to use this but had both of my children take self-defense classes so that they could be prepared.

Shopping safety – Try to go shopping with another person any time you go to the mall or department stores. Make sure you park near the entrance and the lighting is adequate. Be aware of your surroundings. If you think you are being followed go to the nearest store and ask them to call security. If you are uncomfortable walking out to your car ask security if they could escort you. When driving if you think you're being followed don't go home. Drive to the nearest police or fire department. If you are in an area that is not familiar drive to the store or gas station and ask for them to contact the police.

Holidays

I dreaded the holidays. Each holiday and birthday had traditions that are so hard to get through the first year. On top of that I put on two charity bake sales each year at work. We raise funds for the local homeless shelter. From Halloween to Christmas my kitchen turns into a candy and cake shop. With the help of some of my friends at work I was able to have both of the bake sales. I also would get requests from family and friends to make cakes and candies. When my husband was first disabled it was hard for us financially. I came up with this crazy idea to make cakes and teach to bring in some extra income. I had to stop the teaching because I never knew if he was OK or not and it was too much for him to handle. But he loved to cook and I would call him with what cake pan and flavor. I went home each day and the cake would be ready for me to ice when I returned. Without him I scaled down the cakes and candy to just family and friends. Without him I started working on the candy for my bake sale a month ahead of time. It kept me busy each night and helped me get through the first year. I also have a blog, LynnDavisCakes.com that I would post my cakes, candies and craft projects on. I had started it to promote my books but I soon found it was a great way to reach out and post tips on how to make the various cakes and craft projects.

It was time to change traditions and pass on some to my daughter and her family. It was also time to add some new ones.

Halloween

My son loved Halloween. Instead of skipping it I kept myself busy making candy and cakes for a charity bake sale. I found a mold to make chocolate rats. Chris would have loved it. Instead of just plain chocolate candy bars I found a mold to make rat candy bars. I put Chocolate Rice Krispies in the center. They were a hit and it kept me busy and was a great way to work through the holiday. All of the proceeds from the bake sale were donated to the local homeless shelter. I was given a tour and they explained how they get the homeless back on their feet. When I would think about the homeless I never really thought about all of the homeless children. It was heart breaking and it gave me something to focus on besides my own grief. Over the years we have a couple of bake sales a year to raise funds for the shelter.

Working with these people helped me more than I helped them.

Thanksgiving

Thanksgiving was always at my house and last year I decided to change some things up. We had dinner at my daughter's house and early the next morning we all took off to the Grand Canyon for a weekend adventure. My grandson loved the movie the Polar Express. I booked tickets for my daughter, son-in-law, my two grandchildren and myself. It was so completely different then all of the day after Thanksgiving shopping, putting up lights, getting decorations out that we would normally do and we all had a great time. For the kids it was magical. The Grand Canyon Railroad Hotel went all out. There was crafts with Mrs. Claus, the movie was played all day in one of the ballrooms. For the actual ride on the Polar Express train everyone dressed up in their PJ's for the train ride. They served hot chocolate and cookies and read the story of the Polar Express. Half way through the ride the train stopped to pick up Santa. Everyone was told the louder they sang the faster Santa would be there. My son-in-law and another gentleman were trying to out sing each other. It was really funny to watch. When Santa arrived in our rail car he gave each child a bell that had the Polar Express engraved on it. Only the children received the bells but one of Santa's helpers came back to present my son-in-law a bell. She told him that they could hear him in the first car. We were in train car J. It was a wonderful trip and so different than the normal Thanksgiving weekend.

Christmas

Christmas was the hardest of the holidays to get through. Both my son and my husband loved Christmas. My husband would light up our house like the one on Christmas Vacation movie. Even when he had his surgeries and was recover it was something he would look forward to each year. My son-in-law would help and my grandchildren would help me with the tree. Now I had an empty house which was much too quiet and depressing.

Christmas Cards – As hard as it was to do, I sat down and made sure to send them out to my family and friends but also to include a card to all the people that helped me through this terrible time. I had saved the cards from the funeral so that I wouldn't miss anyone.

Holiday Parties – It is OK to turn down parties. It was so hard to be around friends that were having a good time and laughing when you are crying inside. No one will be offended if you turn them down.

Holiday Concerts – Each year my husband would get tickets to Tran Siberian Orchestra. My son died two months before the concert. My husband thought it would be a good idea if we went to the concert to get out of the house. I didn't want to go but what could I say? At the concert they made an announcement that one of their lead singers had passed away. It was one week after my son. That did it, I was in tears for the rest of the concert. If you are not ready then just say no and give the tickets to a family member or friend.

Gifts – I would catch myself shopping for my son and husband each year. Go ahead and buy the gifts and donate it to charity. Each year I organize a bake sale for Halloween and Christmas and made collections of canned goods and food for the Second Harvest. I also organized a clothing drive. Focusing on others helped me get through the holidays.

Special Ornaments – Each year when we put up our Christmas tree we have a special place in the center for loved ones we have lost. I purchased a special frame and put it on the tree with their special ornaments. Last year I decided not to put up the tree but gave the large tree to my daughter with most of the ornaments. It was time to have her take over and I put up two small trees and hung the special ornaments on them.

Valentine's Day

Instead of feeling blue for not having that special someone on Valentine's Day change it up. I bought a candy mold to make chocolate covered Oreos and went to work. With the help of my grandchildren we made the Oreos. I made some chocolate mini hearts that we used to make Valentine trail mix for my friends that included mini chocolate morsels, honey nut trail mix, and Valentine conversation hearts. We made some for each of their friends and had a great time. I played cupid at work and dropped the treat bags on everyone desk very early so that they wouldn't know who was playing cupid. All of the custom candies I made gave it away.

Easter

At work we collected plastic eggs and my co-workers and friends donated candy and toys. Once all of the eggs were filled we took them to the shelter for the children. There were 83 kids that had a lot of fun hunting those eggs.

A hug from an angel – the day before my son's birthday I was very sad. I was given a gift five years ago. I was climbing the stairs and stopped at the top when I felt someone give me a hug. Everything went dark for a second and then my vision returned to normal. I felt such a peaceful feeling like everything was OK in this world. I went to my bed and laid down. At that time I had two kittens who would normally be swinging off the curtains. Both of them sat next to my feet and guarded me all night. The next morning that peaceful feeling went away and I was shaken up when I realized what a special gift I had been given. Each year on their birthdays I know they are in heaven. I keep myself very busy at the office. I also try and not think about the day of their death but celebrate their birthdays instead. Remember them in your heart and be thankful of the times you had together.

Starting Over

After working through the grief it is time to figure out what you want for your future. I took a hard look at myself and saw a middle aged woman that had let herself go. I also found over the last year I missed the interaction even though due to his disability it was only an hour or two a day. I thought I would grow old with him but that was not to be. So at 57 years old I started to take stock of what I wanted in life. I had a small little house that I could afford to keep. I have a good job and lots of friends at work but no one to come home to. No one to share my day, share my dreams or laugh at my latest creation/project. I caught up on all my chick flicks. The upside I only did 2 loads of laundry a week instead of 20. When I came home there wasn't a kitchen full of dirty dishes and the house stayed the same way as I left it. But looking around I wanted to have this place alive again. Oh well what was some extra dishes or laundry when you have someone who will be there to help and share your life with.

The thought of dating again was very scary. Where do I start and who would want a frumpy old housewife. Time to start working towards your future just remember to act your age but that doesn't mean you can't dazzle them even if you have too many curves. It also means you have to unclutter your life, not only emotionally, but also your home.

Diet – Yes we all say we are going to lose weight for their New Year's resolution and that falls flat after the first two weeks. There wasn't much my husband could do but he loved to cook and would get his feelings hurt if I didn't eat everything he made. Believe it or not by just changing my eating habits and trying to eat a healthy meal I lost 20 pounds the first 8 months. That was without trying. The next 20 was going to be hard. Get rid of the snack drawer at work. There are days when I never get out of the office and just work right through. I have started to take my lunch instead of going out with the girls or picking up fast food. Just like any diet your weight will yoyo up and down when you have bad day and there will be some. Chocolate or shopping therapy always help to get through the depression.

Exercise – to help with the new you, add in some exercise to tone up those muscles. Even just taking a 10 minute break at work and walking around the parking lot helps. Get up and move. Join a club or if you are adventurous, try a dance class. I signed up for a ballroom dance class. The lesson was once a week with an open dance every Friday for only $20.00 for one month. I thought this is going to be a breeze. Boy was I wrong. There were two 80 year old men that could dance circles around me. The dance class changed partners every 5 minutes as they showed new steps. I was barely able to keep up the first two weeks. I found one lady who had divorced and was just starting over again. It is a great way to get out of the house and to meet people. The only advice you I can give you is to buy steel toed dance shoes. The first two weeks my toes were so sore that I was limping around work. My friend would tease me and ask how my two 80 year old boyfriends were doing.

Clothes and Shoes - One side effect of losing the weight was my clothes no longer fit. I took a serious look and it was time to clean out and update my wardrobe. Since I work at a manufacturing facility the dress code is casual, jeans and a nice shirt unless we have visitors. Looking though my closet I didn't even have something nice to wear on a date. You don't have to spend a lot of money to update your new look. Each week I would buy a new piece of clothing - a dress, slacks or skirt and don't forget shoes. I keep to the basics colors of black, dark blue, white then add some bright colors to complement. If you are on a tight budget check out your local thrift stores. I have found some designer label shirts for only a few dollars.

Walking in high heels was something that I gave up 25 years ago when my late husband broke my heel by pulling me into a swimming pool. You know that saying you break it you buy it. Well he did, my heel was cracked. Not only did he have to carry me into my apartment so that I could change clothes, but he also had to call my mom to pick up the kids. After three months on crutches I put away the high heels. Looking at my shoes it was time to upgrade them. I bought two pairs of heels. The first pair I wore to an awards dinner. My car was on the other side of the hotel. By the time I got half way the shoes hit the first trash can I found. The second pair I took back. Just like everything else in your life, take baby steps. The next pair was only 1" heels. I will work up to maybe a 2" by summer.

Hair style – Take a good look in the mirror. It doesn't hurt to try out a new color, highlights or even a new style. If you don't like the results then keep changing until you are pleased with what you see.

Finger and Toe Nails – I had given up trying to paint my nails because I was either making cakes or new craft new project so my nails were always chipped, so why bother? I had lots of nail polish but I used it to make Easter or Dinosaur eggs for my Egg Craft for All Ages book. First impressions are everything if you are asked out. It was time to start caring about my appearance again.

Home or Apartment projects - Not only do you need to update yourself but also your home. My home had lots of pictures showing the family. There was also some pictures of his family and a wedding sampler that hung by the front door. I took those pictures and wedding sampler down and put them away.

Re-arranging/updating your furniture – my husband had this old recliner in the living room that was the first thing to go. I tried to tackle one room at a time starting with the living room. When I looked around the room screamed of the life we had together. It doesn't have to cost a lot but slowly I started cleaning out, moving furniture around and making this my space now. Everything that I had wanted to get rid of went in the garage. My daughter came over and helped out with his office. That was the hardest of all. His office had two computers, hundreds of DVD's all out of their cases in digital storage Ducal systems. We found all of the cases in the attic and sat on the floor of his office for two hours sorting out the mess. My husband also liked to make and sell military models and these were everywhere. Some of the models he had built were in display cases and the others were ready to sell on eBay. I started doing some research on the models in order to see what they were worth. He had three submarines that cost $1,000 each. One of the subs he tested in a neighbor's pool. The sub went forward and back, then sank.

Garage Sale - It took a couple of months and my daughter helped me with two different garage sales. The first one was at my house. We picked the hottest weekend of the year. The temperature was 100 in the shade. I had lots of neighbors came by but there were also a lot of guys checking out my garage. One of Jim's friends came to help sell the military model kits. He told a lot of guys about the sale. We also sold some of the tools from my husband's machine shop. Whatever you do don't let anyone go into your house. Several guys made me uncomfortable. Not such a good idea that they all now know I'm by myself. The next garage sale I hauled everything over to my daughter's home which had a community garage sale.

I kept all of the models in the display cases for my grandson. At 5 years old he loved to look at them. My husband made a 4 foot long battleship which I thought had been discarded years ago. I found it in the loft in the garage wrapped in plastic. For Dorian's 6th birthday party the theme was battleship. My daughter took him for a tour of the battleship parked in San Diego, CA. I made the cake and to his surprise I gave him the battleship I found in the garage. It was great to watch Dorian and his friends laying on their stomachs on the living room floor looking at all the details. Watching him I decided that half of the models in the garage would be kept for him.

If you don't know where to start then start with a list of projects. Take your time and tackle one room a month. Set up boxes in your garage; donate, garage sale, trash, books to donate to the Library.

Dating

Now it is time to dive in but how? After being married for 25 years, dating is so completely different now. In high school and college it was easy but now where to start? All the guys I used to date had a full head of hair and had muscles. Now they are balding and those muscles have turned to flab. Going to bars was out. Start with taking stock of what type of person you would like to meet. Be realistic, do you want a drop dead gorgeous guy who might be great for the honeymoon phase of the relationship but then what? Do you want someone who has similar interests? How about starting to look for a new best friend and companion?

Church Groups – The church I attend has singles groups, church socials and even dances. Attending the Sunday services will help you with grief support, and focus on your spiritual journey, give you opportunities to volunteer, as well as meet new people.

Blind Dates – My friends found out I had started to go out again and they wanted to set me up with an older family member. You can lose friends this way so watch out. During parties I would be introduced to older single men. Some were nice but my friends forgot I had already heard about these guys from all of their gossip.

Dating at work – when I'm not writing or making cakes my normal job in the Human Resources department of a medical device company. I have seen too many relationships start then turn sour which makes working together next to impossible. The majority of time one of them will end up quitting.

Ex-husband or old boyfriends – I never thought about my ex-husband until one day I had flowers, candy and a huge three foot tall teddy bear delivered at work. The card was a happy Mother's Day. We had kept in touch because of the kids. His wife had died four months ago and he was relocating back to California. I made the mistake of letting him and his son stay at my home while he was looking for an apartment. I had a week in mind but that kept getting longer and longer until I finally had to put my foot down. My grandson's birthday was later that week so I shoved that huge bear in the car and when my granddaughter saw it she looked at me, "Is that for me?"

My ex-husband had just arrived and I told her to go and ask him. I gave him the old evil eye and he turned and told her it was a special surprise for her. Later that night my daughter looked in on the kids and all she saw of Milena was legs and arms sticking out from under the huge bear. That bear is still being talked about with tons of laughter. My granddaughter likes to surprise her parents and put the bear in front of the window. My daughter got up to go to the bathroom and saw the outline. It scared her to death that it might be an intruder. Then she remembered the bear and laughed. My ex-husband and I went back to being friends again with an understanding no more bears! What I didn't know was that there were pictures of the bear which show up every once in a while.

Dentist Office – You never know when you will meet your future spouse. I met my husband at the dentist's office. I had a root canal and he has a filing when the dentist decided to play match maker. I was never so embarrassed in my life. I had files hanging out of my mouth and drooling. He was numb and could only smile. I couldn't wait to get out of there and never see this guy again. The next week I had told the dentist that my girlfriend was divorced and I was going to take her to a dance club so that she could meet some guys. I completely forgot that I had told the dentist about the dance club until he showed up the next week with my future husband. You just never know when that special someone will come into your life.

Internet Dating - I was talked into trying Internet dating. There are several to choose from, i.e. Parents Without partners, Match.com, Our Time, Christian Mingle, etc. I signed up and immediately I had to fill out what type of guy I was looking for: height, age, range within 25 miles, smoking/non-smoking, status; married, widowed, single, and legally separated. Do they have children and are the children still at home? That was the easy part. You have to fill in the blanks about yourself and write up a something about yourself and what type of person you would like to find for your profile. They also wanted pictures. Since I was always the one on the other side of the camera, I didn't have any current pictures of me. I almost chickened out at this point. I had gotten this far, so I took the camera in the bathroom and started taking pictures with the view finder next to the mirror so I could see my face. I took a couple dozen shots and finally had two to post. OK here goes nothing, I uploaded the pictures and was surprised at the response which was almost immediate. The website sent daily pictures of the gentlemen that fit my wish list.

What you see isn't always what you get. Just because you are honest with your pictures and profile it doesn't mean they will be. I read the profiles and received a response to meet for coffee. When he walked in I had a hard time looking at this guy and remembering the picture. It was like night and day, not even close. Not only did he not look like his picture but he was still living with his wife but they were legally separated. We talked about a half hour and I was never so glad to get out of there. By the way always meet somewhere with lots of people around.

Second try – this guy gave me his number so that we could speak first. When I called he let me know that all of the ladies will need to go through a make-out session first and he did have roaming hands before he would consider taking them out on a date. He also said that I would have to go up to his house and didn't like to meet at public places. I told him thank you for your time but this is not what I was looking for.

Third try – on his profile he had put down that he owned his own business and his hobby is playing bass guitar. We agreed to meet at a small bar not far from my house. I got there and met him. He seemed really nice. He was helping the band set up and would come over and talk to me for a few minutes then went back to help out. Kind of strange but everyone in the band came over to say hello. Now I was really confused but that was cleared up once they started to play and my date was not only playing the bass guitar but also the singer. He would take a break and come over to talk to me for a few minutes. I just wasn't sure of him but I did have a great time and everyone there treated me like a family member. He was a very nice guy, just a little strange but harmless. His business he owned had one employee, him. He would write computer programs in between his musical shows. He had just broke up and didn't want to rebound and only wanted a friend to hang out with. We became friends but nothing more. I think he liked my dog more than me. Besides I am too old to be a groupie.

It didn't take any time at all before I could read the profiles so that I didn't make the same mistakes of the first three dates. I also changed my profile to exclude anyone who was legally separated, no smokers and he has to have children and pets. I am family person and have always had pets. I also had responsibilities and couldn't take off at the drop of a hat to go traveling. Be true to yourself and keep in the back of your mind prince charming is not going to be using an internet website. You are not going to get the best looking guys because they will be checking out the ladies who are 20 years younger than you. I had to realistic, my husband was going bald and had a beer gut. I also had changed over the years.

Waiting for the phone call or text – Dating sucks especially when you wait for that phone just like when I was a teenager. Internet dating is like that. You start emailing from inside the website back and forth then you hear nothing back. After two messages with no return message I would drop it. You don't want to be a stalker.

Dictionary – You might want to have a dictionary on hand when you are reviewing some profiles. I should have paid more attention in English class, here are some new vocabulary words;

- Oenophile – someone who enjoys wine
- Taciturn – shy, reluctant to join in conversation
- Tantric Life style – Used loosely in west to denote erotic spiritualism – sometimes it is better not to ask especially at dinner. The gentlemen had visited a sexual goddess to be evaluated. The good news was he was normal. Wow, that one left me speechless. Time to redirect the conversation. I have

been too sheltered and dating was really strange or at least this one was.

- One gentlemen choose me as his favorite and we started talking via the website internet. He asked me for my regular email so that he wouldn't get in trouble. He said he was in the military and homeland security would not let them sign up for the dating. He also said the profile and pictures was one of his friends and asked again for my direct email address. At this point I had the website block his access to my profile.

Depression - Failed dates had me doubting myself. With each person I would meet I learned not only what type of person they were looking for but what type of person I wanted in my life. It is OK to turn the internet dating off and regroup. Take some time off and do something fun.

Take a class - My daughter surprised me with a wine and painting class. We had some wine and an instructor took us step by step on the painting below. A couple of glasses of wine and my lines were not that straight but it was a lot of fun and I got to meet some really nice people.

This is a chance to fill in some of those things on your bucket list. My daughter and I have taken a cupcake, cookie, two tier cakes, beginning earring making, hat and scarf loom and water color painting classes. Most of these were at JoAnn or Michael's craft stores. Not only will this get you out of the house but this is an opportunity to meet new people.

Family reaction - I also hadn't considered the reaction my daughter would have from me dating again. She was shocked at first then and then was very supportive. It was driving her crazy and she actually told my granddaughter to ask questions about the guy I was seeing and she would take her out for ice cream. When my granddaughter started asking questions when I was watching her that next week, I asked who wanted to know. Milena told me about the deal with her mom. What my daughter didn't count on was that grandma could also bribe her right back. Milena got her ice cream and I made my daughter wait a full week before giving her any details.

Merging families – The hard part of any senior dating is working with both families and their busy schedules. When I look at my schedule I only have 1 or 2 evenings free a week. Between helping out my mother who can no longer get out and about, and spending my time with my grandchildren there is not much free time for dating. Grandchildren are children for such a short time that anytime I get to interact with them is the best part of my week. Having said that, the gentlemen I have gone out with have the same kind of time constraints.

Be a good listener – I have made friends with some older gentlemen who just want to have someone to talk to. One had a stroke and has difficulty speaking. Great guy who only wants a friend to talk to every once in a while.

Texting – I have had to learn all of the acronyms of texting. There are lists on the internet. I also had to upgrade my phone. My old phone was great, I could text and call but that was it. No apps, how did society ever get along without smart phones? This generations uses apps for everything. Looking up directions on a map if you don't have a GPS means you are not cool. Heaven help society if there is a solar flare and everything electronic is temporary shutdown. I think some people have lost the art of communicating with each other. Be careful what you post online especially pictures. Once it is out there it's next to impossible to get back. What is posted on the internet can hurt you for future jobs. Employers are now looking at Facebook pages.

I haven't found Mr. Right yet but I am in no hurry. The best things in life are worth the wait. I am not looking for a drop dead gorgeous guy just someone who would be my companion to share my good and bad days with. Someone who doesn't mind my crazy family, animals and projects. If I can do it, then so can you. You are not alone starting over at this time in your life. There are a lot of us out there just like you.

Best wishes to you and your family as you start the next chapter in your life!

Lynn Davis

For more cake, cupcake, crafts and the latest books please see my blog at LynnDavisCakes.com

Current Books Available on Amazon.com:

Coloring Book Cakes

Sizzling Summer Recipes

Mother's Day – Gifts Made with Love

Mrs. Claus' Cooking Class & Competition

Santa Stories

Gifts Made with Love for Mother's Day

Getting out of the dog house for Father's Day

Ark Journey Series:

The Egg Thieves

Cretaceous Pirates

Pirates Revenge, Stranded in the Cretaceous

Hunting Predators

68077735R00040

Made in the USA
San Bernardino, CA
29 January 2018